HUMAN RESOURCES MANAGEMENT

GHANCHI MAHAMMADHUSHEN
KASAM BHAI

Old No. 38, New No. 6
McNichols Road, Chetpet
Chennai - 600 031

First Published by Notion Press 2019
Copyright © Ghanchi Mahammadhushen kasam bhai 2019
All Rights Reserved.

ISBN 978-1-64678-450-9

This book has been published with all efforts taken to make the material error-free after the consent of the author. However, the author and the publisher do not assume and hereby disclaim any liability to any party for any loss, damage, or disruption caused by errors or omissions, whether such errors or omissions result from negligence, accident, or any other cause.

While every effort has been made to avoid any mistake or omission, this publication is being sold on the condition and understanding that neither the author nor the publishers or printers would be liable in any manner to any person by reason of any mistake or omission in this publication or for any action taken or omitted to be taken or advice rendered or accepted on the basis of this work. For any defect in printing or binding the publishers will be liable only to replace the defective copy by another copy of this work then available.

Contents

1. Concept And Definitions Of Hrm — 1
2. Role Of Hrm Recruitment Process — 12
3. Recruitment Process — 26
4. Human Resource Management Promotions, Transfers And Separations — 31
5. Job Analysis — 45
Reference — 59

CHAPTER ONE

Concept and Definitions of HRM

Concept of HRM

HRM is concerned with the human beings in an organization. "The management of man" is a very important and challenging job because of the dynamic nature of the people. No two people are similar in mental abilities, tacticians, sentiments, and behaviors; they differ widely also as a group and are subject to many varied influences. People are responsive, they feel, think and act therefore they can not be operated like a machine or shifted and altered like template in a room layout. They therefore need a tactful handing by management personnel."

HRM is the process of managing people of an organization with a human approach. Human resources approach to manpower enables the manager to view the people as an important resource. It is the approach through which organization can utilize the manpower not only for the benefits of the organization but for the growth, development and self satisfaction of the concerned people. Thus, HRM is a system that focuses on human resources development on one hand and effective management of people on the other hand so that people will enjoy human dignity in their employment.

HRM is involved in providing human dignity to the employees taking into account their capacity, potentially, talents, achievement, motivation, skill, commitment, great abilities, and so on. So, that their personalities are recognized as valuable human beings. If an organization can trust, depend and draw from their bank account on the strength of their capital assets, they can trust, depend and draw more on their committed, talented, dedicated and capable people. This is what the HRM is involved in every business, managerial activity or introduction.

The principal component of an organization is its human resource or 'people at work'.

According to Leon C. Megginson from the national point of view Human Resources as, "the knowledge, skills, creative abilities, talents and aptitudes obtained in the population; whereas from the . view point of the individual enterprise, they represent the total of inherent abilities, acquired knowledge and skills as exemplified in the talents and

aptitudes of its employees."

Human resource has a paramount importance in the success of any organization because most of the problems in organizational setting are human and social rather than physical, technical or economical failure. In the words of Oliver Shelden, "No industry can be rendered efficient so long as the basic fact remains unrecognized that it is principally human."

Human Resources Management is concerned with the "people" dimension in management. Since every organization is made up of people acquiring their services, developing their skills, motivating them to high level of performance and ensuring that they continue to maintain their commitment to the organization are essential to achieve

organizational objectives. This is true regardless of the type of organization, government, business, education, health, recreation or social action. Getting and keeping good people is critical to the success of every organization, whether profit or non-profit, public or private.

Definitions of HRM

There are two different definitions. The first definition of HRM is that "It is the process of managing people in organizations in a structured and thorough manner." This covers the fields of staffing (hiring people), retention of people, pay and perks setting and management, performance management, change management and taking care of exits from the company to round off the activities. This is the traditional definition of HRM which leads some experts to define it as a modem version of the Personnel Management function that was used earlier.

The second definition of HRM encompasses "The management of people in organizations from a macro perspective, i.e. managing people in the form of a collective relationship between management and employees." This approach focuses on the objectives and outcomes of the HRM functions. It means that the HR function in contemporary organizations is concerned with the notions of people enabling, people development and a focus on making the "employment relationship" fulfilling for both the management and employees.

In simple words, Human resource management is management function that helps manager to recruit, select, train and develop organization members. Or HRM is a process of making the efficient and effective use of human resources so that the set goals are achieved.

In general terms, Human Resource Management is "concerned with the people dimension in management. Since every organization is made up of people, acquiring their services, developing their skills, motivating them to high levels of performance and ensuring that they continue to maintain their commitment to the organization are essential

for achieving organizational objectives. This is true regardless of the type of organization government business, Education, Health, regression or social action."

In the words of **Dunn and Stephens,** "The HRM is the process of attracting, holding and motivating all manager line and staff."

The National Institute of Personnel Management (NIPM) of India has defined human resource as "that part of management which is with people at work and with their relationship within an enterprise. Its aim is to bring together and develop into an effective organization of the men and women who make up an enterprise and having regard for the well-being of the individuals and of working groups, to enable them to

make their best contribution to its success."

Scope of HRM

The scope of HRM is indeed vast. All major activities in the working life of a worker - from the time of his or her entry into an organization until he or she leaves the organization comes under the preview of HRM. The major HRM activities include HR planning, job analysis, job design, employee hiring, employee and executive remuneration, employee motivation, employee maintenance, industrial relations and of HRM. The scope of Human Resources Management extends to:

> All the decisions, strategies, factors, principles, operations, practices, functions, activities and methods related to the management of people as employees in any type of organization.

> All the dimensions related to people in their employment relationships and all the dynamics that flow from it. American Society for Training and Development (ASTD) conducted fairly an exhaustive study in this field and identified nine broad areas of activities of HRM.

Scope of HRM

These are given below:
- ❖ Human Resource Planning
- ❖ Design of the Organization and Job
- ❖ Selection and Staffing
- ❖ Training and Development
- ❖ Organizational Development

- ❖ Compensation and Benefits
- ❖ Employee Assistance
- ❖ Union/Labour Relations
- ❖ Personnel Research and Information Systema)

Human Resource Planning: The objective of HR Planning is to ensure that the

organization has the right types of persons at the right time at the right place. It prepares human resources inventory with a view to assess present and future needs, availability and possible shortages in human resource. Moreover, HR Planning forecast demand and supplies and identify sources of selection. HR Planning develops strategies both long term and short-term, to meet the man-power requirement.

b) Design of Organization and Job: This is the task of laying down organization structure, authority, relationship and responsibilities. This will also mean definition of work contents for each position in the organization. This is done by :'job description". Another important step is "Job specification". Job specification identifies the attributes of persons who will be most suitable for each job which is defined by job description.

c) Selection and Staffing: This is the process of recruitment and selection of staff. This involves matching people and their expectations with which the job specifications and career path available within the organization.

d) Training and Development: This involves an organized attempt to find out training needs of individuals to meet the knowledge and skill which is needed not only to perform current job but also to fulfill the future needs of the organization.

e) Organizational Development: This is an important aspect whereby "Synergetic effect" is generated in an organization i.e. healthy interpersonal and inter-group relationship within the organization.

f) Compensation and Benefits: This is the area of wages and salaries administration where wages and compensations are fixed scientifically to meet fairness and equity criteria. In addition labour welfare measures are involved which include benefits and services.

g) Employee Assistance: Each employee is unique in character, personality, expectation and temperament. By and large each one of them faces problems everyday. Some are personal some are official. In their case he or she remains worried. Such worries must be removed to make him or her more productive and happy.

h) Union-Labour Relations: Healthy Industrial and Labour relations are very important for enhancing peace and productivity in an organization. This is one of the areas of HRM.

i) Personnel Research and Information System: Knowledge on behavioral science and industrial psychology throws better insight into the workers expectations, aspirations and behavior. Advancement of technology of product and production methods have created working environment which are much different from the past.

Globalization of economy has increased competition many fold. Science of ergonomics gives better ideas of doing a work more conveniently by an employee. Thus, continuous research in HR areas is an unavoidable requirement. It must also take special care for improving exchange of information through effective communication systems on a continuous basis especially on moral and motivation. HRM is a broad concept; personnel management (PM) and Human resource development (HRD) are the parts of HRM.

Nature of HRM

HRM is a management function that helps managers to recmit, select, train and develop members for an organization. HRM is concerned with people's dimension in organizations. The following aspects constitute the core of HRM:

1. HRM Involves the Application of Management Functions and Principles. The functions and principles are applied for acquiring, developing, maintaining and providing remuneration to employees in organization.

2. Decision Relating to Employees must be integrated. Decisions on different aspects of employees must be consistent with other human resource (HR) decisions.

3. Decisions Made Influence the Effectiveness of an Organization. Effectiveness of an organization will result in betterment of services to customers in the form of high quality products supplied at reasonable costs.

4. HRM Functions are not confined to Business Establishments Only but applicable to non-business organizations such as education, health care, recreation and like.

HRM refers to a set of programmes, functions and activities designed and carried out in order to maximize both employee as well as organizational effectiveness

Objectives of HRM

The primary objective of HRM is to ensure the availability of competent and willing workforce for an organization. Beyond this, there are other objectives too. Specifically, HRM objectives are four fold: Societal, Organization, Functional and personal.

• Personal Objectives:
To assist Employees in achieving their personal goals, at least in so far as these goals enhance the individual's contribution to the organization. Personal objectives of employees must be maintained, retained and motivated.

Objectives of HRM

Functional Objectives:

To maintain the contribution of department at an appropriate level organization should fulfill the needs. Resources are wasted when HRM is either more or less sophisticated to suit the organizations demands.

• Organizational Objectives:

To recognize the role of HRM in bringing about organizational effectiveness, HRM is not an end in itself but it is only a mean to assist the organization with its primary objectives organization.

- **Societal Objectives:**

To be ethically & socially responsible for the needs and challenges of society while minimizing the negative impact of such demands upon the organization to use their resources for society's benefits in ethical ways may lead to restriction.

- **Other objectives:**

^ Accomplish the basic organizational goals by creating and utilizing an able and motivated workforce.

v" To establish and maintain organizational structure and desirable working relationships among all the members of the organization.

S Develop co-ordination among individual and group within organization to secure the integration of organization.

S To create facilities and opportunities for individual or group development so as to match it with the growth of the organization.

S To attain an effective utilization of human resources in the achievement of organizational goals.

S To identify and satisfy individual and group needs by providing adequate and equitable wages, incentives, employee benefits and social security and measures for challenging work, prestige, recognition, security, status.

S To maintain high employees morale and human relations by sustaining and improving the various conditions and facilities.

S To strengthen and appreciate the human assets continuously by providing training and development programs.

•S To consider and contribute to the minimization of socio-economic evils such as unemployment, under employment, inequalities in the distribution of income and wealth and to improve the welfare of the society by providing employment opportunities to women and disadvantaged sections of the society.

■/ To provide an opportunity for expression and voice management.

■S To provide fair, acceptable and efficient leadership.

S To provide facilities and conditions of work and creation of favorable atmosphere for maintaining stability of employment.

To create & utilize an able & motivated work force Establish & maintain sound organizational structure Create facilities attain an effective utilization Identify & satisfy individual & group needs.

v" Maintain high employee morale Training & development Opportunity for expression Provide fair, acceptable and efficient leadership Facilities and conditions.

CHAPTER TWO

Role of HRM Recruitment process

Role of HRM

The role of HRM is to plan, develop and administer policies and programs designed to make optimum use of an organizations human resources. It is that part of management which is concerned with the people at work and with their relationship within enterprises.

Current Classification of HR roles:

According to R.L Mathis and J. H. Jackson (2010) several roles can be fulfilled by HR management. The nature and extent of these roles depend on both what upper management wants HR management to do and what competencies the HR staff have demonstrated. Three roles are typically identified for HR.
- Administrative
- Operational Actions
- Strategic HR

1. Administrative Role of HR:

The administrative role of HR management has been heavily oriented to administration and recordkeeping including essential legal paperwork and policy implementation. Major changes have happened in the administrative role of HR during the recent years. Two major shifts driving the transformation of the administrative role are: Greater use of

technology and Outsourcing. Technology has been widely used to improve the administrative efficiency of HR and the responsiveness of HR to employees and managers. Moreover; HR functions are becoming available electronically or are being done on the Internet using Web-based technology. Technology is being used in most HR activities, from employment applications and employee benefits enrollments to e-laming using Internet-based resources.

Classification of HR Roles

Administrative

Personnel practices
Legal compliance forms
and paperwork

Operational Actions

Managing employee
relationship issues
Employee advocate

This outsourcing of HR administrative activities has grown dramatically in HR areas such as employee assistance (counseling), retirement planning, benefits administration, payroll services and outplacement services.

2. Operational and Employee Advocate Role for HR:

HR managers manage most HR activities in line with the strategies and operations that have been identified by management and serves as employee "champion" for employee issues and concerns.

HR often has been viewed as the "employee advocate" in organizations. They act as the voice for employee concerns, and spend considerable time on HR "crisis management," dealing with employee problems that are both work-related and non work-related. Employee advocacy helps to ensure fair and equitable treatment for employees regardless of personal background or circumstances. Sometimes the HR's advocate role may create conflict with operating managers. However, without the HR advocate role, employers could face even more lawsuits and regulatory complaints than they do now. The operational role requires HR professionals to co-operate with various departmental and operating managers and supervisors in order to identify and implement needed programs and policies in the organization. Operational activities are tactical in nature. Compliance with equal employment opportunity and other laws are ensured, employment applications are processed, current openings are filled through interviews, supervisors are ained, safety problems are resolved and wage and benefit questions are answered. For

carrying out these activities HR manager matches HR activities with the strategies of the organization.

Strategic Role for HR:

The administrative role traditionally has been the dominant role for HR. A broader transformation in HR is needed so that significantly less HR time and fewer HR staffs are used just for clerical work. Differences between the operational and strategic roles exist in a number of HR areas. The strategic HR role means that HR professionals are proactive in addressing business realities and focusing on fiiture business needs, such as strategic planning, compensation strategies, the performance of HR and measuring its results. However, in some organizations, HR often does not play a key role in formulating the strategies for the

organization as a whole; instead it merely carries them out through HR activities. Many executives, managers, and HR profession ls are increasingly seeing the need for HR management to become a greater strategic contributor to the business success of organizations. HR should be responsible for knowing what the true cost of human capital

is for an employer. For example, it may cost two times key employees' annual salaries to replace them if they leave. Turnover can be controlled though HR activities, and if it is successful I saving the company money with good retention and talent management strategies, those may be important contributions to the bottom line of organizational performance. The role of HR as a strategic business partner is often described as "having a seat at the table," and contributing to the strategic directions and success of the organization. That means HR is involved in devising strategy in addition of implementing strategy. Part of

HR's contribution is to have financial expertise and to produce financial results, not just to boost employee morale or administrative efficiencies. Therefore, a significant concern for chief financial officers (CFOs) is whether HR executives are equipped to help them to plan and meet financial requirements.

The role of HR shifted from a facilitator to a functional peer with competencies in other functions and is acknowledged as an equal partner by others. The HR is motivated to contribute to organizational objectives of profitability and customer satisfaction and is seen as a vehicle for realization of quality development. The department has a responsibility for monitoring employee satisfaction, since it is seen as substitute to

customer satisfaction.

According to McKinsey's 7-S framework model HR plays the role of a catalyst for the organization. According to this framework, effective organizational change is a complex relationship between seven S's.

HRM is a total matching process between the three Hard S (Strategy, Structure and Systems) and the four Soft S (Style, Staff, Skills and Super-ordinate Goals). Clearly, all the S's have to complement each other and have to be aligned towards a single corporate vision for the organization to be effective. It has to be realized that most of the S's are determined directly or indirectly by the way Human Resources are managed and therefore, HRM must be a part of the total business strategy.

Importance of HRM

The importance of human resource management can be discussed by Yodder, Heneman and others, from three standpoints, *viz.,* social, professional and individual enterprise.

1. *Social Significance:* Proper management of personnel enhances their dignity by satisfying their social needs.

This is done by: *(i)* maintaining a balance between the jobs available and the jobseekers, according to the qualifications and needs

(ii) Providing suitable and most productive employment, which might bring them psychological satisfaction; *(iii)* making maximum utilization of the resources in an effective manner and paying the employee a reasonable compensation in proportion to the contribution made by him; *(iv)* eliminating waste or improper use of human resource, through conservation of their normal energy and health; and *(v)* by helping people make their own decisions, that are in their interests.

2. *Professional Significance-*

By providing healthy working environment it

promotes team work in the employees. This is done by: *(i)* maintaining the dignity of the employee as a 'human-being'; *(ii)* providing maximum opportunity for personal development; *(Hi)* providing healthy relationship between different work groups so that work is effectively performed; *(iv)* improving the employees' working skill and capacity; *(v)* correcting the errors of wrong postings and proper reallocation of work.

3. ***Significance for Individual Enterprise:*** It can help the organization in accomplishing its goals by: *(i)* creating right attitude among the employees through effective motivation; *(ii)* utilizing effectively the available goals of the enterprise and fulfilling their own social and other psychological needs of recognition, love, affection, belongingness, esteem and self-actualization.

Dynamic and growth - oriented organization do require effective management of people in a fast - changing environment. Organizations flourish only through the efforts and competencies of their human resources. Employee capabilities must continuously be acquired, sharpened, and used. Any organization will have proper human resource management *(i)* to improve the capabilities of an individual; *(ii)* to develop team spirit of an individual and the department; and *(Hi)* to obtain necessaiy co - operation from the employees to promote organizational effectiveness.

Functions of HRM

Human Resources management has an important role to play in equipping organizations to meet the challenges of an expanding and increasingly competitive sector. Increase in staff numbers, contractual diversification and changes in demographic profile which compel the HR managers to reconfigure the role and significance of human resources management.

The functions are responsive to current staffing needs, but can be proactive in reshaping organizational objectives.

All the functions of HRM are correlated with the core objectives of HRM . For example personal objectives are sought to be realized through functions like remuneration, assessment etc. HR management can be thought of as seven interlinked functions taking place within organizations, as depicted in Figure below. Additionally, external forces—legal, economic, technological, global, environmental, cultural/geographic, political, and social—significantly affect how HR functions are

designed, managed, and changed.

RECRUITMENT AND INTRODUCTION

The overall aim of the recruitment and selections process is to obtain the right number and quality of employee's required to satisfy the human resources need of the organisation.

The four stages of recruitment and selection are:

1. Defining requirements:

preparing job descriptions and specification, deciding terms and conditions of employment,

2. Attracting candidates:

reviewing and evaluating alternative sources for applicants, inside and outside the organization, advertising, possibly using agencies and consultants.

3. Selecting candidates:

sifting applications, interviewing, testing, assessing candidates, employment, taking references, employment contract

4. Introduction- induction:

Introduction to the work and the colleagues, to the organization and its main objectives, to terms of employment.

Each of the stages will be described more in detail below.

Defining requirements
Requirements Attracting
candidates
Recruitment
Selecting candidates
Appointing employee
Introduction of employee
Requirements
Attracting candidates
Recruitment
Selecting candidates
Appointing employee
Introduction of employee
Job description/Job analysis

Defining the requirements is based on what the job description says about the content of the job and what the job specification says about the requirements in order to compile the content of an internal announcement or and external advertisement regarding the specific recruitment. It is important to check that the job description is up-to-date and accurately expresses the present requirements.

Defining the requirements also includes decisions about

▶ Are the tasks permanent or non-permanent?
▶ Is the job permanent or non-permanent?
▶ Which legal form of employment shall be applied?

Attracting candidates

The question about where to find candidates is partly a formal legal issue. There might be legal provisions about internal announcement within the specific ministry before it is allowed to advertise publicly. There might be provisions

There are often some form of internal announcement within the public

administration before external advertisements may be used. Furthermore, there might be provisions that make advertisement in certain ways compulsory. The content of an internal announcement shall basically have the same content as an external advertisement.

Advertising

The main purpose of a job advertisement is to attract all candidates that are suitable for the job and only those. Therefore, the advertisement shall stimulat the suitable candidates to apply for the job and at the same time tell persons that are not suitable that they would be unsuccessful. The advertisement shall make it possible for the readers to asses if they are suitable for the specific job or not. Comprehensive and accurate description of the job and its requirement will make this possible.

Requirements attracting candidates
Recruitment
Selecting candidates
Appointing employee
Introduction of employee
Where to find candidates?
How to attract them?

Check the advertisement against the following check-list

· The work organisation - its main occupation and location

· The job - its title, main duties, location

· Qualifications and experience- personal requirements, special

professional qualification, experience, aptitudes etc.

· Rewards and opportunities - basic salary and other emoluments, other

benefits, opportunities for personal development, if any

· Training that may be given

· Conditions - any special factors and circumstances affecting the job

· Applications - forms of application, closing date etc

· The design and the content must be attractive. Advertisement is a way to

market the organisation.

· Do not overburden with unnecessary information and use a nonbureaucratic language

· Make it possible to seek additional information by contacting the

organisation.

Selecting candidates

Requirements Attracting candidates

Recruitment

Selecting candidates

Appointing employee

Introduction of employee

Competent?

Motivated?

Fitting in?

Selecting people aims at finding a person who can meet the requirements described in the job description and job specification. It is difficult to get the right people into the organisation but even harder to get the wrong people out from the organisation, especially in public service organisations. Mistakes in selecting candidates can have very serious consequences for the effectiveness of the organisation.

Three basic questions are vital for a successful recruitment

1. Can the candidate do the job - is he/she competent?
2. Will the candidate do the job - is he/she motivated?
3. How will the candidate fit into the organisation?

In order to provide answers to these questions, the selection process must not be mechanical.

There might be formal legal provisions as well as policies about how the selection process should be carried out and organised. The process must comply with such provisions and policies.

The selection of candidates is generally based on information about the

candidates from

- ▶ Documents provided by candidates
- ▶ Interviews
- ▶ Selection tests
- ▶ Previous employers

For the public administration, there might be provisions of law or regulations stating that only applications that have arrived before the closing date may be taken into consideration.

When all the applications have been received by the due date, the next task is to select those applicants who appear to be the most suitable for the job. This task will be based on the published requirements for the job and involves a critical study of the information provided by applicants, a comparison of this information with job requirements and, finally a decision whether to accept or reject on this stage. It is normally useful to carry out a preliminary sift to place the applicants in three categories

1. suitable,
2. not suitable and
3. possible.

Those responsible for processing applications need to be aware throughout, that they (1) have a *responsibility to their employer* to be as careful and thorough as possible in selecting the most suitable candidate and that they (2) have a responsibility to the applicants themselves to examine their applications conscientiously and fairly. The selection task is important and difficult in general terms and in the following, a few of the requirements for a successful selection are listed.

· Awareness of the essential nature of the task and its inherent problems.

· Clear and comprehensive definitions of the criteria for effective

  performance

· Thorough training / briefing for selectors to make them aware of the

  inherent problems and to develop necessary skills for effective practice,

  for example training in interviewing skills.

· A follow up system to check how well the predictions made in the

  selection process have turned out in practice.

The next step of the process aims at finding the *most suitable* candidate among the group of suitable persons found through the preliminary sifting.

CHAPTER THREE

Recruitment process

The selection interview

recruitment process. This means that it is made clear in advance whether interviews shall beused or not, how many candidates that should be interviewed and how theinterview shall be organised.An interview can be described as a conversation with a purpose. It is aconversation because candidates should be induced to talk freely with their interviewers about themselves, their experience and their careers. But theconversation has to be planned, directed and controlled to achieve the mainpurpose of the interview, which is to make an accurate prediction of thecandidate's coming performance in the job for which he or she is beingconsidered. It is also important to use considered yardsticks or list of questionswhen interviewing many for the same job, to compare the findings from theinterviews. The selection interview is also a valuable opportunity for an exchangeof information, which will enable both parties to make a decision. To offer or notto offer a job, to accept or not to accept the offer.

Interviews

- A single one-to-one interview
- A series of one-to-one interviews at the end of which interviewers

compare views and discuss final conclusions.

- A board or panel interview with a group of interviewers
- A combination of one-to-one and board interviews

Whatever method is selected, it is important that the interviewee is at ease and that the method ensures that all positive as well as negative factors are fully exposed. The requirements for the job are always the basic checklist for the interview.

Selection tests

Selection tests are used to provide more valid and reliable evidence of levels of intelligence, personality, characteristics, abilities, aptitudes and attainments than can be obtained from an interview.

Psychological test

A psychological test can be defined as a carefully chosen, systematic and standardized procedure for evolving a sample of responses from candidates, which can be used to assess one or more of their psychological characteristics with those of a representative sample of an appropriate population.

Intelligence tests

Intelligence tests measure general intelligence.

Personality tests

Personality tests assess the personality in order to make prediction about their likely behaviour in a role

Ability tests

Ability tests measure job-related characteristics such as number, verbal, perceptual or mechanical ability

Aptitude tests

Aptitude tests are job-specific test that are designed to predict the potential an individual has to perform within a job*Attainment tests*

Attainment tests measure abilities or skills that have already been acquired by

training or experience, ex typing test

The above serves as a general guidance and explanation of various tests.

Specialists must be used for each type or approach.

Tests usually provide important and complementary information about

applicants, and, if applied, should be used within the overall framework of methods and information required in the specific case linked to the specific requirements of each job. A wide and general use of tests to ensure that only suitable candidates will be admitted is normally not worth the cost and the time involved. Tests should be used only for candidates that by other means are considered suitable.

The meaningfulness of test should also be considered in relation to the type of job (for example low level routine jobs) and the type of employment (for example temporary employments).

Taking references

The purpose of the reference from previous employers is to obtain information about a candidate and opinions about his or her personality and how he or she will fit for the new job. The factual information is essential. It is important to confirm the nature of the previous job and other facts, for example time of employment, how the candidate performed, his/her strong and weak side etc. It is normal to take references from 2-3 previous employers. Telephone references is a good way to get information The great advantage of a telephone conversation is that people are more likely to give an honest opinion orally than if they have to commit themselves in writing. Written references are another good way, while personal references may have less value.

In some culture it is regarded as unfair to collect information about a candidate in this way. Be cautious of attempts by previous and present employers to give good references in order to get rid of the person

1. Learning Outcome

After completing this module the students will be able to:

? Understand the meaning of Promotion, demotion, transfer and separations.

? Know the advantages and disadvantages of promotion, demotion and transfer.

? Know the policy and bases of promotion.

? Understand the meaning of quits, layoffs, discharges, retirements, retrenchments, VRS and Resignation.

2. Introduction

Internal mobility is the process of movement of employees which takes place between the jobs in sections, departments or divisions of the organization. Internal

Mobility is necessary to match the employee's skill and requirements with the requirements of the job and those of the organization continuously. The objectives of internal mobility are:

- to improve organizational effectiveness

- to eliminate structural defects and unwanted positions

- to improve employee effectiveness by putting his knowledge, skills and abilities to better use

- to adjust to changing business operations

- to ensure discipline

- to correct wrong placements and job assignments

Internal mobility can take any or more of the form of promotion, demotion, transfer.

CHAPTER FOUR

Human Resource Management Promotions, transfers and separations

Management Human Resource Management Promotions, transfers and separations

Promotion

Promotion is an upward movement of employee in the organization to another job, higher in organisation's hierarchy. In the new job, the employee finds a change in salary, status, responsibility and grade of job or designation. As a whole, the organization perceives the staffing of vacancy worth more than the employee's present position. In contrast to promotion when the salary of an employee is increased without a corresponding change in the job-grade, it is known as 'upgrading'. But when promotion does not result in change in pay, it is called 'dry promotion'. Promotion is a method of internal mobility.

Principles of Promotion

Promotion is a double edged weapon. If handled carefully, it contributes to employee satisfaction and motivation. If mishandled, it leads to discontentment and frustration among the employees.

Policy of promotion

The HRM must make it clear whether to fill up higher positions by internal promotions or recruit people from outside. Generally speaking top positions in an organisation are filled through external recruitment. The lower positions are filled by promotions from within.

When it has been decided to fill up higher positions with promotions, a further decision on determining the basis of promotion should be made by HRM. The basis of promotion may be seniority or merit or both.

One most important point regarding the policy of promotion is whether to promote employees against vacancies or non-vacancies. In many organizations promotions are done on a non-vacancy basis after they complete a minimum period of service. Such promotions are time bound and not based on vacancies or merit. The other practice is to link promotions to vacancies. Sometimes these vacancies are created to avoid frustration among the aspirants for promotion.

A promotion should be preceded by a job analysis and performance appraisal. A job analysis is important to know what the job demands from the employee and performance appraisal will enable the management to know whether the employee in question can match the requirements of the job.

The promotion policy should be discussed with the labour unions and their acceptance must be obtained in the form of an agreement.

When promotions are made on the basis of competence, openings for promotion should be displayed at several places to enable interested people to apply.

Bases of promotion

Organisations adopt different bases of promotion depending on their nature, size, managerial policy etc. The well established bases of promotion are seniority and merit.

Seniority based promotion

If seniority is the bases for promotion, an employee with the longest period of service will get promoted, irrespective of whether he is competent or not.

Ø Advantages

? It is easy to administer.

? It is easy to measure the length of service and judge the seniority.

? With the base of seniority there is no scope for favoritism, discrimination and subjective judgement.

? By seniority everyone is sure of getting promotion one day.

? Subordinates are more willing to work under an older boss who has given many years of service to the company.

Ø **Disadvantages**

? The learning capabilities of senior (older) employees may diminish.

? It de-motivates the younger and more competent employees and it results in more employee turnover.

? The organisation is deprived of external talent which is very necessary due to technological advancements and multi-culture organisation.

? Judging the seniority is highly difficult as the problems like job seniority, company seniority, regional seniority, service in different organizations, trainee experience, research experience etc., will crop up.

Merit or competence based promotion

Merit based promotion occur when an employee is promoted because of superior performance in the current job. Merit means an individual's knowledge, skills, abilities as measured from his educational qualifications, experience, training, and past employment record.

Ø **Advantages**

? Promotion by merit is a reward to encourage those employees who make a successful effort to increase their knowledge or skill and who maintain a high level of productivity.

? It helps the employer to focus on talented employees recognize their talent and reward their contributions.

? Efficiency is encouraged, recognized and rewarded.

? Competent people are retained as better prospects are open to them.

? It inspires other employees to improve their standards of performance through active participation in all activities and putting in more efforts.

Ø Disadvantages

? It is not easy to measure merit. Personal prejudices, biases, and union pressures may come in the way of promoting the best performer.

? When young employees get ahead of senior employees in the organization this creates frustration among senior employees .They feel
insecure and may alsos quit the organization.

The past performance may not guarantee future success of an employee.

? Loyalty and length of service is not properly rewarded

Advantages of Promotion Plan

• It provides an opportunity to the present employees to move into jobs that provide greater personal satisfaction and prestige.

• It offers opportunities to management to provide recognition and incentives to the better employees, to correct initial mistakes in appointments and to 'freeze' inefficient personnel.

• It generates within an organization beneficial pressures on work performance and desired behaviour of all its members.

• It serves as an orderly, logical and prompt source of recruitment for management to fill vacancies as they arise.

• Promotion fulfils the long cherished desires in the lives of employees.

Disadvantages of Promotion Plan

• Promotion promotes "inbreeding" in which the company will not have new blood and new thinking. Old habits and ideas are perpetuated.

• The system becomes stagnant, repetitious and very conventional.

• The newer employees are introduced at places where they are having little influence.

Demotion

Demotion is the reverse of promotion. It is the downward movement of an employee in hierarchy with lower status, salary and decreased responsibilities. It is generally used as a punitive measure for incompetence or a preliminary step to dismissal. It is a downgrading process where the employees suffer considerable emotional and financial loss.

Causes for demotion

? The employee may be unable to meet the challenges posed by a new job.

? He may have low administrative skills.

? Due to poor business conditions and continuous losses, a firm may decide to layoff some and to downgrade others.

? It is sometimes used as a disciplinary tool against offending employees.

Transfer

A transfer implies a lateral movement of an employee in the hierarchy of positions with the same pay and status. Transfers may be either company initiated or employee initiated. In fact, a transfer is a change in job assignment. It may involve a promotion, demotion or no change at all in status and responsibility.

Transfers from one job to another may be either temporary or permanent. Temporary transfers may be due to

- temporary absenteeism
- shifts in the workload
- vacations

Permanent transfers may be due to

- shifts in the workload
- vacancies requiring the special skill of the transferred employee
- ill-health of the employee

Transfer requests might come from the worker himself, from his superior, from the head of another department or may be made necessary by changes in the volume of trading activities. When the transfer request comes from the employee himself, it is because he does not like the work or the place of work or the co-workers.

Requests for transfers should be favourably considered especially when it comes from an employee. An unsatisfied employee is more of a liability than an asset. It is true that no company can comply with all requests for transfers.

Production transfer

Transfers from jobs in which labour requirements are declining to jobs in which they are increasing (through resignation or otherwise) are called production transfer.

This type of transfer is made to avoid lay-off of efficient employees by providing them with alternative positions in the same organisation.

— Improve employee satisfaction

— Improve employee-employer relations.

Problems with transfers

— Inconvenient to employees.

— Employees may or may not fit in the new location

— Shifting of experienced hands may affect productivity

— Discriminatory transfer may affect employee satisfaction.

Employee separation

Employee separation occurs when employees cease to be a member of an organization. Agreement between employer & employee comes to an end. Employees decide to leave the organization or organization ask employee to leave. Reasons for employee separations are voluntary or involuntary. In the former initiation for separation is taken by employee himself or herself. Where the employer initiates to separate an employee it becomes involuntary separation.

Retirements
Voluntary Separations
Quits

An employee decides to quit when his or her level of dissatisfaction with the present job is high or a more alternative job is awaiting the individual. Organisations often encourage quits through cash incentives. Popularly known as voluntary retirement scheme (VRS) these schemes are offered by the organizations when they are experiencing losses. They resort to cost saving and believe that the best way of cost saving is to cut the wages of the employees. As VRS are induced by the management it comes under involuntary separations.

Voluntary Separations

Quits

An employee decides to quit when his or her level of dissatisfaction with the present job is high or a more alternative job is awaiting the individual. Organisations often encourage quits through cash incentives. Popularly known as voluntary retirement scheme (VRS) these schemes are offered by the organizations when they are experiencing losses. They resort to cost saving and believe that the best way of cost saving is to cut the wages of the employees. As VRS are induced by the management it comes under involuntary separations.

Retirements

Retirements occur when employees reach the end of their careers. The age for an employee's superannuation differs. Retirement differs from quits. When the employee superannuates and leaves the organization, he or she carries several benefits with himself or herself. Such a privilege is denied to the employee who quits.

Second, retirement occurs at the end of an employee's career but the quit can take place at any time.

Third, superannuation shall not leave any bad relationship behind the retiree but a quit is likely to result in hurt feelings with the employer.

Involuntary Separations

Employers resort to terminate employment contract with employees for at least three reasons:

? Organization is passing through lean period and is unable to maintain the existing labour

? Initial faulty hiring resulting in mismatch between job and employee.

? Employee exhibits unusual behavior making the environment ineffective.

Discharges, layoffs, retrenchment and VRS are the common methods of employer sponsored separations.

Discharge or Dismissal

A discharge takes place when the employer discovers that it is no more desirable to keep an employee any longer. Discharge, also called termination, should be avoided as far as possible. Termination is expensive as the firm must seek replacement, hire and train the new hiree. A discharged individual is likely to badmouth about the company. Dismissal is the last step and may be resorted to when all the efforts in salvaging the employee have failed. The following reasons lead to the dismissal of an employee:

? Excessive absenteeism

· Serious misconduct

? False statement of qualification at the time of employment

? Theft of company property

Layoff

A layoff is a temporary separation of the employee at the instance of the employer. Section 2(kkk) of **The Industrial Disputes Act, 1947**, defines layoff as *"the failure, refusal or inability of an employer to give employment to a worker whose name is present on the rolls but who has not been retrenched"*. A layoff may be for a definite period on the expiry of which the employee will be recalled by the employer for the duty.

As the employees are laid off by the employer they have to be paid compensation for the period they are laid off. Section 25 of **The Industrial Disputes Act, 1947** makes it compulsory for the employer to pay compensation for all the days of layoff. The compensation must be equal to half of the normal wages the employee would have earned if he or she would not have been laid off.

A layoff may be for one of the following reason:

? Shortage of coal, power or raw materials

? Accumulation of stocks

? Breakdown of machinery etc.

Retrenchment

It refers to the termination of the employee because of the replacement of labour by machines or the closure of a department due to continuing lack of demand of the products manufactured in that particular department of the organisation. If the plant is itself closed then the management and the employees have to leave for good. Like layoff retrenchment also entitles the employees to compensation which in terms of section 25(f) of the industrial disputes act, 1947 is equivalent to 15 days average pay for every competed year of continuous service.

Retrenchment however differs from layoff in the sense that in layoff the employee continues to be in the employment of the organization and is sure to be recalled after the end of the period of layoff whereas, in retrenchment, the employee's relation with the company are detached immediately.

Retrenchment also differs from dismissal. An employee is dismissed due to his or her own fault and dismissal is usually done of one or two employees whereas retrenchment is forced both on the employer and the employee and it involves the termination of several employees.

Voluntary retirement scheme

Beginning in the early 1980's, companies both public and private sector have been sending home surplus labour for good reasons not by retrenchment but by a novel scheme called Voluntary retirement scheme VRS also *shake plan*". Handsome compensation is paid to the leaving employees.

VRS is thought to be painless and time saving method of trimming the staff strength and getting rid of unproductive older workers. Many organizations like Hindustan Lever, Siemens, TISCO have successfully operated this scheme and achieved great success.

Resignation

A resignation refers to the termination of employment at the instance of the employee in that case it is voluntary but if forced by the employer for not putting his duty well ,or for some serious charge against him than it becomes involuntary. An employee may resign when he or she gets a good job elsewhere, or due to ill health, or may resign due to some personal problems

CHAPTER FIVE

Job Analysis

Following definitions will help you to understand the concept of job analysis better:

A defined data collection and analysis procedure through which information about job tasks and job requirements are obtained.

Job analysis is the procedure for determining the duties and skill requirements of a job and the kind of person who should be hired for it.

Organizations consist of positions that have to be staffed. Job analysis is the procedure through which you determine the duties of these positions and the characteristics of the people who should be hired for them .The analysis produces information on job requirements, which is then used for developing job descriptions (what the job entails) and job specifications (what kind of people to hire for the job).

Now let us go through the 6 Steps In Job Analysis

Go through the following six steps in doing a job analysis. They will make the concept clear to you.

Step 1

Identify the use to which the information will be put, since this will determine the types of data you collect and how you collect them. Some data collection techniques like interviewing the employee and asking what the job entails and what his responsibilities are - are good for writing job

Identify how information will be used 1
Review background information 2
Select representative positions to analyse 3
Collect data to analyse job 4
Review information with incumbents 5
Develop Job Description / Job Specification 6
Step 2

Review relevant background information such as organization charts, process charts, and job descriptions. Organization charts show how the job in question relates to other jobs and where it fits in the overall organization. The chart should identify the title of each position and, by means of its interconnecting lines, show who reports to whom and with whom the job incumbent is expected to communicate.

Step 3

Select representative positions to be analyzed. This is done when many similar jobs are to be analyzed and it is too time-consuming to analyze, say, the jobs of all assembly workers.

Step 4

Next actually analyze the job by collecting data on job activities, required employee behaviors, working conditions, and human traits and abilities needed to perform the job. For this, you would use one or more of the job analysis techniques explained in this lesson.

Step 5

Review the information with job incumbents. The job analysis information should be verified with the worker performing the job and with his or her immediate supervisor. This will help to confirm that the information is factually correct and complete. This "review" step can also help gain the employee's acceptance of the job analysis data and conclusions by giving that person a chance to review and modify your description of his or her job activities.

Step 6

Develop a job description and job specification. A job description and a job specification are usually two concrete products of the job analysis. The job description is a, written statement that describes the activities and responsibilities of the job, as well as important features of the job such as working conditions and safety hazards. The job specification summarizes the personal qualities, skills, and background required for getting the job done; it may be either a separate document or on the same document as the job description.

It is very important to understand why is Job Analysis required:

? What is Job Analysis - job analysis is obtaining information about jobs.

? Why is Job Analysis important - Without sufficient knowledge of what employees do, organizations cannot develop other human resource practices and procedures.

Job analysis is a systematic procedure for studying jobs to determine their various elements and requirements. The job analysis for a particular position typically consists of two parts.

o A job description is a list of the elements that make up a particular job.

o A job specification is a list of the qualifications required to perform particular job.

Job Description Vs. Job Specification

o **Job Description** - written narrative describing activities performed on a job; includes information about equipment used and working conditions under which job is performed.

o **Job Specification** - outlines specific skills, knowledge, abilities, physical and personal characteristics necessary to perform a job - What about physical and personal characteristics? Strength, patience, intestinal fortitude, risk-taker.

It is essential for you to understand that Job Analysis helps to find information about the following:

Work activities. Information is usually collected on the actual work activities performed, such as cleaning, selling, teaching, or painting. Such a list may also indicate how, why, and when the worker performs each activity.

Human behaviors. Information on human behaviors like sensing, communicating, decision-making, and writing may also be collected. Included here would be information regarding human job demands such as lifting weights, walking long distances, and so on.

Machines, tools, equipment, and work aids used. Included here would be information regarding products made, materials processed, knowledge dealt with or applied (such as finance or law), and services rendered (such as counseling or repairing)

Performance standards. Information is also collected regarding performance standards (in terms of quantity, quality, or speed for each job duty, for instance) by which an employee in this job will be evaluated.

Job context. Included here is information about such matters as physical working conditions, work schedule, and the organizational and social context-for instance, in terms of the number of people with whom the employee would normally have to interact. Also included here might be information regarding incentives for doing the job.

Human requirements. Finally, information is usually compiled regarding human requirements of the job, such as job-related knowledge or skills (education, training, work experience) and required personal attributes (aptitudes, physical characteristics, personality, interests).

Types Of Information Gathered
Work Activities
- Work activities performed
- How, why, when activity is performed

Human Behaviours
- Communicating, decision making, and
- Other physical job demands, e.g., lifting

Tools, equipment, etc used

- Products made
- Knowledge dealt with / applied
- Servicesrendered

Performance standards
- Quantity, quality, speed
- Used to evaluate employee performance

Let us now have a look at the areas in which Job Analysis Information is used

? **Recruitment and Selection**

Job analysis provides information about what the job entails and what human characteristics are required to carry out these activities. Such job description and job specification information is used to decide what sort of people to recruit and hire.

? **Compensation**

Job analysis information is also essential for estimating the value of and appropriate compensation for each job. This is so because compensation. (such as salary and bonus) usually depends on the job's required skill and education level, safety hazards, degree of responsibility and so on-all factors that are assessed through job analysis. Job analysis provides the information determining the relative worth of each job so that each job can be classified.

? **Ensure Complete Assignment of Duties**

The job analysis is also useful for ensuring that all the duties that have to be done are in fact assigned to particular positions. For example, in analyzing the current job of your company's production manager, you may find she reports herself as being responsible for two dozen or so specific duties including planning weekly production schedules, purchasing raw materials, and supervising the daily activities of each of her first-line supervisors. }v fissing, however, is any reference to managing raw material or finished goods in-

Job Context
- Physical work conditions
- Work group
- Incentives for doing job

Human Requirements
- Job-related knowledge, skills
- Personal attributes, e.g. personality, aptitudes

ventories. On further investigation you find that none of the other manufacturing people is responsible for inventory management either. Your job analysis (based not just on what employees report as their duties, but on your knowledge of what

? **Training**

Job analysis information is also used for designing training and development programs because the analysis and resulting job description show the skills-and therefore training-that are required.

? **Performance Appraisal**

A performance appraisal compares each employee's actual performance with his or her performance standards. It is often through job analysis that experts determine the standards to be achieved and the specific activities to be performed.

JOB ANALYSIS = Process of defining jobs in terms of tasks, behaviors and personal requirements.

Job Analysis
Job Descriptions
Recruiting
Selection
Performance Appraisal
Training
Career Planning

Methods of Collecting Job Analysis Data

You should know that a variety of methods are used to collect information about jobs. None of them, however, is perfect. In actual practice, therefore, a combination of several methods is used for obtaining job analysis data. These are discussed below.

1) **Job performance**: In this method the job analyst actually performs the job in question. The analyst, thus, receives first hand experience of contextual factors on the job including physical hazards, social demands, emotional pressures and mental requirements. This method is useful for jobs that can be easily learned. It is not suitable for jobs that are hazardous (e.g., fire fighters) or for jobs that require extensive training (e.g., doctors, pharmacists).

2) **Personal observation**: The analyst observes the worker(s) doing the job. The tasks performed, the pace at which activities are done, the working conditions, etc., are observed during a complete work cycle. During observation, certain **precautions** should be taken

? The analyst must observe average workers during average conditions.

? The analyst should observe without getting directly involved in the job.

? The analyst must make note of the specific job needs and not the behaviours specific to particular workers.

? The analyst must make sure that he obtains a proper sample for generalisation.

Compensation

Job Evaluation

This method allows for a deep understanding of job duties. It is appropriate for manual, short period job activities. On the negative side, the methods fail to take note of the mental aspects of jobs.

3) **Critical incidents:** The critical incident technique (CIT) is a qualitative approach to job analysis used to obtain specific, behaviorally focused descriptions of work or other activities. Here the job holders are asked to describe several incidents based on their past experience. The incidents so collected are analysed and classified according to the job areas they describe. The job requirements will become clear once the analyst draws the line between effective and ineffective behaviours of workers oh the job. For example, if a shoe salesman comments on the size of a customer's feet and the customer leaves the store in a huff, the behaviour of the salesman may be judged as ineffective in terms of the result it produced. The critical incidents are recorded after the events have already taken place - both routine and non-routine. The process of collecting a fairly good number of incidents is a lengthy one. Since, incidents of behaviour can be quite dissimilar, the process of classifying data into usable job descriptions can be difficult. The analysts overseeing the work must have analytical skills and ability to translate the content of descriptions into meaningful statements.

4) **Interview:** The interview method consists of asking questions to both incumbents and supervisors in either an individual or a group setting. The reason behind the use of this method is that jobholders are most familiar with the job and can supplement the information obtained through observation. Workers know the specific duties of the job and supervisors are aware of the job's relationship to the

rest of the organisation.

Due diligence must be exercised while using the interview method. The interviewer must be trained in proper interviewing techniques. It is advisable to use a standard format so as to focus the interview to the purpose of analyst.

Guidelines for Conducting Job Analysis Interviews

o Put the worker at ease; establish rapport.

o Make the purpose of the interview clear.

o Encourage the worker to talk through empathy.

o Help the worker to think and talk according to the logical
sequence of the duties performed. .

o Ask the worker only one question at a time.

o Phrase questions carefully so that the answers will be more than just "yes" or" no".

o Avoid asking leading questions.

o Secure specified and complete information pertaining to the work performed and the worker's traits

o Conduct the interview in plain, easy language.

o Consider the relationship of the present job to other jobs in the department.

o Control the time and subject matter of the interview.

o Be patient and considerate to the worker.

o Summarise the information obtained before closing the interview.

o Close the interview promptly.

Although the interview method provides opportunities to elicit information sometimes not available through other methods, it has limitations. First, it is time consuming and hence costly. Second, the value of data is primarily dependent on the interviewer's skills and may be faulty if they put ambiguous questions to workers. Last, interviewees may be suspicious about the motives and may distort the information they provide. If seen as an opportunity to improve their positions such as to increase their wages, workers may exaggerate their job duties to add greater weightage to their positions.

5) **Questionnaire method:** The questionnaire is a widely used method of analysing jobs and work. Here the jobholders are given a properly designed questionnaire aimed at eliciting relevant job-related information. After completion, the questionnaires are handed over to supervisors. The supervisors can seek further clarifications on various items by talking to the jobholders directly. After everything is finalised, the data is given to the job analyst.

The success of the method depends on various factors. The structured questionnaire must cover all job related tasks and behaviours. Each task or behaviour should be described in terms of features such as importance, difficulty, frequency, and relationship to overall performance. The jobholders should be asked to properly rate the various job factors and communicate the same on paper. The ratings thus collected are then put to close examination with a view to find out the actual job requirements.

Questionnaire method is highly economical as it covers a large number of job holder" at a time. The collected data can be quantified and processed through a computer. The participants can complete the items leisurely. Designing questionnaires however is not an easy task. Proper care must be taken to see that the respondents do He': misinterpret the questions. Further, it is difficult to motivate the participants to complete the questionnaires truthfully and to return them.

Let us now have a look at some of the standard questionnaires that are being widely used. They are discussed below for your better understanding:

1. The Position Analysis Questionnaire (PAQ)

The PAQ is a standardised questionnaire (developed at Purdue University) developed to quantitatively sample work-oriented job elements. It contains 194 items divided into six major divisions. The PAQ permits management to scientifically and quantitatively group interrelated job elements into job dimensions. These are explained below:

Employees Activities in PAQ

1. **Information Input:** Where and how does the employee gets the information he/she uses in performing his/her job.

Examples:

Use of written materials.

Near-visual differentiation.

2. **Mental Process:** What reasoning, decision making, planning and information-processing activities are involved in performing in the job?

Examples:

Levels of reasoning in problem solving.

Coding/decoding

1. **Physical activities:** What physical activities does the employee perform and what tools or devices does he/she use?

Examples:

Use of Keyboard devices.

Assembling/ disassembling.

2. **Relationships with other people:** What relationships with other people are required in performing the job?

Examples:

Instructing, Contacts with public, customers.

3. **Job context:** In what physical and social context is the work performed?

Examples:

High temperature.

Interpersonal conflict situations.

4. **Other Job characteristics:** What activities, conditions, or characteristics other than those described above are relevant to the job?

Examples:

Specified work pace.

Amount of job structure.

The activities shown above represent requirements that are applicable to all types of jobs. This type of quantitative questionnaire allows many different jobs to be compared with each other.

2. **Management Position Description Questionnaire (MPDQ)**

MPQD is a standardised instrument designed specifically for use in analyzing managerial jobs. The 274-item questionnaire contains 15 sections. It would take 21\2hrs to complete the questionnaire. In most cases the respondents are asked to state how important each item is to the position.

Reference

www.google.com

www.shodhaganga.com

www.hrm.com

www.ingramcontent.com/pod-product-compliance
Lightning Source LLC
Chambersburg PA
CBHW021026180526
45163CB00005B/2136